To Mum: I'm hungry, I'm tired, I'm cold, I'm hot, Can I have..., Where are you?

To Dad: Where's Mum?

"If evolution really works, how come Mothers only have two hands?"

What's the difference between Superman and Mothers?

Superman's just a superhero now and then. Mums are superheroes all the time.

My nickname is Mom.

*But my full name
is "Mom Mom Mom Mom Mom."*

**Mother: (noun) One person who
does the work of 20. For free.**

What did mommy spider say to
baby spider?

*You spend too much time on the
web.*

Son: "Mom can I get twenty bucks"
Mom: Does it look like I am made of money?

Son:
"Well isn't that what M.O.M stands for?"

What did the baby corn say to the mama corn?

"Where's Popcorn?"

Daughter: "Mom, I need my personal space!"

Mom: "You came out of my personal space."

A police recruit was asked during the exam, "What would you do if you had to arrest your own mother?"

He said, "Call for backup."

What are the best type of flowers for a boy to buy his Mom for Mother's Day?

Son flowers.

Why did the cookie cry?

Because his mother was a wafer so long!

What do you call a small mom?

Minimum.

What did the mama tomato say to the baby tomato?

Catch up!

Why don't mothers wear watches?

There's a clock on the stove.

Why did the baby strawberry cry?

Because his mom was in a jam!

What did the momma horse say to the foal?

Its pasture your bedtime

What did the mother broom say to the baby broom?

It's time to go to sweep!

Mom, what's it like to have the greatest daughter in the world?

I don't know dear, ask your grandmother.

"If at first you don't succeed...try doing it the way Mom told you to in the beginning."

What did the Panda give his mommy?

A bear hug.

What kind of coffee was the alien mommy drinking?

Starbucks.

Why was it so hard for the pirate to call his mom?

Because she left the phone off the hook.

What did the lazy boy say to his mom on Mother's Day when she was about to do the dishes?

Relax mom... you can just do them in the morning.

What kind of sweets do astronaut moms like?

Mars bars.

What was Cleopatra's favorite day of the year?

Mummy's day.

Nothing is really lost...until mom can't find it.

What did the baby Egyptian say when he got lost?

I want my mummy.

Science teacher: When is the boiling point reached?

Student: When my mother sees my report card!

What makes more noise than a child jumping on mommy's bed?

Two children jumping on mommy's bed!

Why did mom get a plate of English muffins?

Her family wanted her to feel like a queen!

Why did the boy put the Mother's Day cupcakes in the freezer?

His sister told him to ice them.

What's the best thing a new mom can get for Mother's Day?

A long nap.

Why was mom so happy to go to IHOP for pancakes on Mother's Day?

She knew she wouldn't have to do any dishes.

Where did the reindeer family go for ice cream on Mother's Day?

Deery Queen.

Son: Mommy, how does breakfast in bed sound to you?

Mommy: It sounds wonderful!

Son: Great... I'll have scrambled eggs, pancakes and hashbrowns.

There is a legend that says if you take a shower and scream out loud "Mom" three times, a nice lady appears bringing the towel you forgot.

"Having kids makes you look stable to the people who thought you were crazy and crazy to the people who thought you were stable."

Yes, please get a new cup every time you need water — said no mom ever.

Knock Knock.
Who's there?
Omelet.
Omelet who?

Omelet Mommy sleep in today.

Knock, knock
Who's there?
Annie
Annie who?

Annie thing you can do, Mum can do better.

Silence is golden.
Unless you have kids
Then silence is suspicious.

Licked a dark smear off my finger, and then thought,

"Phew it's chocolate."

I don't want to sleep like a baby.

I want to sleep like my husband.

I hate when I'm waiting for mom to cook dinner...

Then I remember that I am the mom and I have to cook dinner.

Whoever wrote the song "Easy Like Sunday morning" did not have kids.

When your mom's voice is so loud, even your neighbors brush their teeth and get dressed.

You know you're a mom when picking up another human to smell their butt isn't only normal but necessary.

I stubbed my toe and my Mom shouted at me for yelling "What the duck!"

She was angry that I used fowl language.

What kind of flowers are best for Mother's Day?

Mums.

"Sleep at this point is just a concept, something I'm looking forward to investigating in the future."

Why did the mommy cat want to go bowling?

She was an alley cat.

What color flowers do mama cats like to get?

Purrrrrrrple flowers.

What warm drink helps mom relax?

Calm-omile tea.

How do you keep little cows quiet so their mommy can sleep late?

Use the moooooote button.

Why did the mommy horse want to race on a rainy day?

She was a mudder.

Why was the house so neat on Mother's Day?

Because Mom spent all day Saturday cleaning it.

"I love when the kids tell me they're bored. As if the lady standing in front of a sink full of dirty dishes is where you go to get ideas about how to have a good time."

"Remember when you first became a parent. And everything was so terrifying? Now you watch your kid lick the grocery cart and you don't even break a sweat."

"I want my children to have all the things I couldn't afford. Then I want to move in with them."

"Children are like crazy, drunken small people in your house."

"Twelve years later the memories of those nights, of that sleep deprivation, still make me rock back and forth a little bit. You want to torture someone? Hand them an adorable baby they love who doesn't sleep."

"When can we come see the baby?"

"4 am would be super helpful, Thanks."

"I just watched my child individually pick off and eat every sprinkle on the donut I gave her."

She has the patience for that, but can't wait 30 seconds for me to pee by myself."

"Kids are challenging. Wine is necessary. They're great though,"

"Raising a kid is part joy and part guerilla warfare."

"I love to play hide and seek with my kid, but some days my goal is to find a hiding place where he can't find me until after high school."

You know you're a mom when you understand why Mama Bear's porridge was too cold.

Cleaning with kids in the house is like brushing your teeth with Oreos.

Happy Mother's Day to someone who spoils me and then complains about how spoiled I am.

"It is never easy being a mother. If it were easy, fathers would do it."

Son: When is Mother's Day Dad? Dad wearily unplugging the vacuum.

"Every day son, every day."

One of my friends is pregnant and I'm really excited.

Not because she's gonna be a mom, but because she's one of my skinniest friends.

Bought my Mum a mug which says, "Happy Mother's day from the World's Worst Son".

I forgot to mail it but I think she knows.

"People who say they sleep like a baby don't have one."

Nick: Why is a computer so smart?

Mom: It listens to its motherboard.

Son: "Mum, stop making jokes you're not funny."

Mum: "I made you."

"I saw Mummy asking Santa why he didn't put his dishes in the dishwasher."

Sunday school teacher: Tell me, Johnny. Do you say prayers before eating?

Johnny: No, ma'am, I don't have to. My Mum's a good cook.

What three words solves Dad's every problem?

Ask your mother.

What's the hardest thing your mother makes you swallow?

The fact they're always right.

The family were disappointed with their Mother's Day celebrations on the moon.

The food was terrific but the restaurant lacked atmosphere.

Mother: Why is there a strange baby in the crib?

Daughter: You told me to change the baby.

How do your kids know that you're upset with them?

You use their full name.

Elephant: Why do mother kangaroos hate rainy days?

Hippo: I give up.

Elephant: Because their kids have to play inside!

What did the mother rope say to her child?...

"Don't be knotty."

What did the digital clock say to its mother?...

"Look, Ma! No hands!"

Joker: Why did the monster's mother knit him three socks?

Harvey: I have no clue.

Joker: She heard he grew another foot!

Erin: What did the mother bullet say to the daddy bullet?

Fran: What?

Erin: "We're gonna have a BB!"

Ryan: Why did you chop the joke book in half?

John: Mom said to cut the comedy.

Son: Dad, do you know the difference between a pack of cookies and a pack of elephants?

Dad: No.

Son: Then it's a good thing Mom does the grocery shopping!

Doug: I think my mom's getting serious about straightening up my room once and for all.

Dan: How do you know?

Doug: She's learning to drive a bulldozer.

Logic: "If you fall off that swing and break your neck, you can't go to the store with me."

Humor: "When that lawn mower cuts off your toes, don't come running to me."

Justice: "One day you'll have kids, and I hope they turn out just like you. Then you'll see what it's like!"

A mother mouse and a baby mouse are walking along when suddenly a cat attacks them. The mother mouse shouts "BARK!" and the cat runs away. "See?" the mother mouse says to her baby.

"Now do you see why it's important to learn a foreign language?"

<u>7 Things Mum Would Never Say</u>

"Yeah, I used to skip school a lot, too."

"Just leave all the lights on ... it makes the house look more cheery."

"Let me smell that shirt — Yeah, it's good for another week."

"Go ahead and keep that stray dog, honey. I'll be glad to feed and walk him every day."

"Well, if Jason's mamma says it's OK, that's good enough for me."

"The curfew is just a general time to shoot for. It's not like I'm running a prison around here."

"Don't bother wearing a jacket – the wind-chill is bound to improve."

Texting Mom Part 1

Texting acronyms can stump even the best parents:

Mom: Your great-aunt just passed away. LOL.

Son: Why is that funny?

Mom: It's not funny, David! What do you mean?

Son: Mom, LOL means Laughing Out Loud.

Mom: I thought it meant Lots of Love. I have to call everyone back.

Texting Mom Part 2

<u>More acronyms with mom</u>:

Daughter: I got an A in Chemistry.

Mom: WTF!

Daughter: Mom, what do you think WTF means?

Mom: Well That's Fantastic.

Mom: What do IDK, LY & TTYL mean?

Daughter: I don't know, love you, talk to you later.

Mom: OK, I will ask your brother.

__Funny Mom Story #1__

For weeks a six-year-old lad kept telling his first-grade teacher about the baby brother or sister that was expected at his house.

One day the mother allowed the boy to feel the movements of the unborn child.The six-year old was obviously impressed, but made no comment. Furthermore, he stopped telling his teacher about the impending event.

The teacher finally sat the boy on her lap and said, "Tommy, whatever has become of that baby brother or sister you were expecting at home?"

Tommy burst into tears and confessed,

"I think Mummy ate it!"

<u>Funny Mom Story #2</u>

A little girl asked her mum, "How did the human race appear?"
Mum answered, "God made Adam and Eve and they had children, and all mankind was made." Two days later the girl asked her Dad the same question. Dad answered, "Many years ago there were monkeys from which the human race evolved."
The confused girl returned to her mum and said, "Mum, why is it that you told me the human race was created by God, and Dad said they developed from monkeys?" The mother answered,

"Well, dear, it is very simple,
I told you about my side of the family
and your father told you about his!"

__Funny Mom Story #3__

One day, a little girl is sitting and watching her mother do the dishes at the kitchen sink. She suddenly notices that her mother has several strands of white hair sticking out in contrast to her brunette hair.

She looks at her mother and inquisitively asks: "Why are some of your hairs white, Mum?" Her mother replied: "Well, every time that you do something wrong and make me cry or unhappy, one of my hairs turns white."

The little girl thought about this revelation for a while and then asked:

"Mumma, how come all of grandma's hairs are white?"

Funny Mom Story #4

Two children ordered their mother to stay in bed one Mother's Day morning.

As she lay there looking forward to breakfast in bed, the smell of bacon floated up from the kitchen.

But after a good long wait she finally went downstairs to investigate. She found them both sitting at the table eating bacon and eggs.

"As a surprise for Mother's Day,"
one explained, "We decided to cook our own breakfast."

Printed in Great Britain
by Amazon